LANG *v.* ANDERSON

LANG *v.* ANDERSON

Second Edition

Anthony J. Bocchino
Jack E. Feinberg Professor of Litigation
Temple University Beasley School of Law

Joseph J. Kalo
Professor of Law
University of North Carolina

Kelly S. Thomas
Attorney at Law
Midland, Texas

NATIONAL INSTITUTE FOR TRIAL ADVOCACY

Address inquiries to:

Reprint Permission
National Institute for Trial Advocacy
1685 38th Street, Suite 200
Boulder, CO 80301-2735
Phone: (800) 225-6482
Fax: (720) 890-7069
E-mail: permissions@nita.org

ISBN 978-1-55681-741-0
FBA 0741

Printed in the United States of America

ASPEN PUBLISHING

Official co-publisher of NITA.
aspenpublishing.com/NITA

TABLE OF CONTENTS

Page

Preface vii

Special Instructions for Use as a Trial 1

Complaint 3

Answer 5

Statute 7

Newspaper Article 9

Deposition of Jeffery B. Lang 11

Deposition of T. J. Johnson 15

Deposition of Susan Clark 17

Deposition of Jennifer L. Anderson 19

Deposition of Philip D. Turner 21

Medical Bills 27

Hospital Report 31

Letter from Employer 35

Diagram 37

Mr. Gatsby's Poster 39

Mr. Gatsby's Advertisement 41

Interrogatories to Defendant 43

Arrest Record of Jeffery B. Lang 45

Arrest Record of Philip D. Turner 47

Arrest Record of Jennifer L. Anderson 49

Memorandum of Law 51

Proposed Jury Instructions 53

Jury Verdict Form #1 (Liability and Damages) 57

Jury Verdict Form #2 (Liability) 59

Jury Verdict Form #3 (Special Verdict) 61

PREFACE

This file is dedicated to the University of North Carolina 1982 National Championship basketball team, which provided all of us here with a great deal of excitement and pleasure. Except for the game described in the file and the excitement it generated, everything is a product of our imagination. There were no fights in any local drinking establishment and no lawsuits. We hope that anyone using this file enjoys it as much as we enjoyed writing it. We wish to thank Alice N. Moseley of the class of 1985 for helping complete the file.

Joseph J. Kalo
Kelly S. Thomas
Chapel Hill, North Carolina
September 12, 1983

I'm a Duke fan, so for me, there are more national championships to remember. I was pleased, however, to update the fine work of my good friend and colleague Joe Kalo and his co-author, Kelly Thomas, for this second edition.

Tony Bocchino
Philadelphia, Pennsylvania
Spring, 2001

SPECIAL INSTRUCTIONS FOR USE AS A TRIAL

This file is intended to be used for a bench trial or a short jury trial. The trial may be limited to the issue of liability; however, we have included adequate materials to allow the issue of damages to also be tried. Each side should be permitted to call only two witnesses. The witnesses for the plaintiff are:

Jeffrey B. Lang
T. J. Johnson

The witnesses for the defendant are:

Jennifer L. Anderson
Susan Clark

All years in these materials are stated in the following form:

- YR-0 indicates the actual year in which the case is being tried (i.e., the present year);
- YR-1 indicates the next preceding year (please use the actual year);
- YR-2 indicates the second preceding year (please use the actual year); etc.

All the depositions were taken in August and September YR-1, the year prior to the time of the trial.

The portion of the Nita University student paper, which appears on page 41, contains Mr. Gatsby's advertisement. The paper was published on March 29, YR-1, and distributed to all Nita University students that morning. It consisted of eight pages. The Mr. Gatsby's 1/8 of a page advertisement appeared on page 2 of the paper.

Required stipulations: The newspaper articles, the advertisement, medical bills, hospital report, letter from plaintiff's employee, photograph, diagram, and arrest records are authentic and admissible in the discretion of the trial judge.

In the state of Nita, a blood-alcohol content of .10 percent creates a presumption of intoxication for the purposes of the offense of driving under the influence of drugs or alcohol and for public intoxication.

Certified medical records are admissible in evidence unless there is a substantial question as to their authenticity pursuant to NGS 13-1316 (A).

Butch Turner is not available to be called as a witness, but relevant portions of his deposition may be introduced in evidence at trial, if admissible. Dr. Phillip Tromper is dead.

In the Circuit Court of
Darrow County, Nita
Civil Division

Jeffrey B. Lang, Plaintiff, vs. Jennifer L. Anderson, doing business as Mr. Gatsby's Defendant	))))))))	<u>Complaint</u> CA-5837

Plaintiff for his Complaint against the Defendant alleges:

1. That at all times hereinafter mentioned, Plaintiff was, and still is, a resident of Nita City, Darrow County, Nita.

2. That Defendant was and still is a resident of Nita City, Darrow County, Nita.

3. That Defendant is the sole owner and operator of a restaurant, Mr. Gatsby's, located at 413 Jefferson Street, Nita City, and that Mr. Gatsby's is licensed to serve beer and wine on its premises.

4. That on March 29, YR-1, Defendant's employees sold and served beer, in large amounts, to Butch Turner, which he consumed on the premises.

5. That as a result of the beer consumed at Mr. Gatsby's, Butch Turner became highly intoxicated.

6. While still in this intoxicated condition Butch Turner hit the plaintiff several times, knocking him to the floor.

7. That as a direct result of Butch Turner's beatings, the plaintiff suffered physical and mental pain and suffering.

8. That as a direct result of Butch Turner's beatings, the plaintiff was medically treated for a broken rib, bruised ligaments, and a hairline fracture. The plaintiff was hospitalized for two days. The plaintiff was unable to work, under doctor's orders, for two months.

9. That as a result, the plaintiff incurred reasonable expenses for medical and hospital care.

10. That as a result, the plaintiff incurred a loss of wages for two months.

Wherefore, Plaintiff demands judgment against the Defendant in a sum sufficient to compensate him for his injuries and losses, together with the cost of this action, and for all other just and proper relief.

Jury Demand

Plaintiff demands a trial by jury in this action.

Harrison and Black
by

[signature]

Attorney for Plaintiff
Suite 1221, Nita Bank Building
Nita City, Nita

Return on Summons

I hereby certify that the above complaint was personally served on Jennifer L. Anderson, at her office in Mr. Gatsby's, 413 Jefferson Street, Nita City, Nita.

James Bell
James Bell
Speedy Subpoena & Process, Inc.

DATED: May 5, YR-1

In the Circuit Court of
Darrow County, Nita
Civil Division

Jeffrey B. Lang,	)	
Plaintiff,	)	
vs.	)	Answer
	)	CA-5837
Jennifer L. Anderson,	)	
doing business	)	
as Mr. Gatsby's	)	
Defendant.	)	

Defendant for his answer to Plaintiff's Complaint:

1. Admits the allegations contained in paragraphs 1–3.

2. Admits that beer was served to Butch Turner by defendant's employees but denies all other allegations in paragraph 4.

3. Denies allegations contained in paragraph 5.

4. Defendant is without sufficient information or knowledge to form a belief as to the truth of the allegations contained in paragraphs 6–10.

Affirmative Defense

5. The plaintiff provoked a fight with Butch Turner in which the plaintiff suffered physical and mental injuries.

Wherefore, Defendant demands that judgment be entered in favor of the Defendant with the costs and disbursements of this action.

Smith, Rhodes and Davis
by

Attorneys for Defendant
First Nita National Bank Plaza
Nita City, Nita

DATED: May 14, YR-1

Certificate of Service

I hereby certify that a copy of the above Answer was placed in the United States mail, postage prepaid, addressed to the law firm of Harrison and Black, Suite 1221, Nita Bank Building, Nita City, Nita.

Maxine Robinson
420 Main Street
Nita City, Nita

Nita General Statutes Title 23 Section 211

Dramshop Act

Every person who is injured in person or property or otherwise by any intoxicated person, has a right of action in his own name, severally or jointly, against any person, who by selling or giving alcoholic liquor, causes the intoxication of such person. Any person owning, renting, leasing, or permitting occupation of any building or premises with knowledge that alcoholic liquors are to be sold therein, or who having leased the same for other purposes, shall knowingly permit therein the sale of any alcoholic liquors that have caused the intoxication of any person, shall be liable, severally or jointly, with the person selling or giving the liquors. In order for the party to be liable pursuant to this statute, the intoxicated person must have been visibly intoxicated at the time the person was served, sold, or given intoxicating beverages by the party so charged.

It shall be a defense to a cause or motion under this Title if the party claiming injury at the hands of an intoxicated person provoked the intoxicated person to act in such a manner as to cause the complained of injuries.

Warrior Fans Celebrate Miracle Victory

by Sally Smith
Nita Times

NITA CITY—The morning after the University of Nita's (Nita U) National Collegiate Championship, Jefferson Street showed all the signs of the campus celebration. The party continued until four this morning, leaving toilet papered trees, gutters filled with beer bottles, and painted messages on buildings, sidewalks, streets, and even campus landmarks.

Police stationed in the campus area Monday night estimated that twenty thousand fans filled the four blocks of Jefferson Street which had been barricaded to contain the crowd. Many of the fans had spent Monday afternoon and evening at the college bars and restaurants.

Local tavern owners reported capacity crowds during the game. But minutes after the final buzzer, the fans poured out of the bars, dormitories, and fraternity houses to celebrate in the street.

The crowd for the most part was easy to control. NPD Officer Tim Mathers said that the fans were just excited. "A few of the students were rather drunk and rowdy, but we pretty much let them have their fun. We just tried to make the celebration as safe as possible."

Police chief John Sloan said that some arrests were made of those fans who were caught damaging property. About twenty drivers were charged with driving under the influence. One woman went into labor and had to be carried from the crowd to University Hospital.

This morning, Nita City Sanitation crews began the clean up. Five truckloads of garbage were hauled away by noon. Local businesses which had anticipated the crowd by covering storefronts were spared a paint job.

Other businesses were not so lucky. Jennifer Anderson, owner of Mr. Gatsby's Restaurant, was one of those hardest hit by the crowd. Her restaurant was filled with students watching the game on three large screen TV's. After the game, the students threw glasses and plates on the floor, turned tables over, and even punched holes in the walls in the post-game excitement.

"I'm just as happy for the team as the students are," said Anderson, "but I'm disappointed with the fans' damage after the game."

DEPOSITION OF JEFFREY B. LANG*

My name is Jeffrey B. Lang. I was born on January 15, YR-22, in Nita City, Nita. My legal residence is with my parents at 4809 Pine Street, Nita City, Nita. I am a senior at the University of Nita, finishing up a degree in business administration. I went to the Nita City public schools and graduated from Nita City High School in YR-5. I decided to enroll at Nita U. because I knew that the school had a good business program. I took off from school for a year in between my sophomore and junior years to earn some money and to think about changing majors. I decided to go back and finish in business. I should graduate in January of YR+1. I have been working at Simpson's, a local restaurant and bar, for about a year part-time.

I am a big sports enthusiast. I've always enjoyed college basketball at Nita U., partly because I played basketball in high school, and especially because our college team is so good. For the last four years, our team has won the conference championship. We even got to the championship game of the NCAA's my freshman year. We lost the game—it was a real heartbreaker. That's why the whole town was excited in March of last year. Our team was really going strong and had beaten Conwell University to get to the NCAA finals. The final game was Monday, March 29, YR-1, against our arch rival, the Wildcats of Nita State University (State).

My classes had been cancelled all day that Monday because of the game. I didn't have to work at Simpson's, either. Some friends from school and I planned on watching the game at Mr. Gatsby's, a pizza and beer place on Jefferson Street across from the Nita U. campus. Gatsby's was the place to be in Nita City that night. Not only did the place have big screen television, but there were plenty of tables and a special price on pitchers of Bud that night. People also wanted to be at Gatsby's because of its location—on Jefferson Street, right across from campus. Four years before, the police blocked off five blocks of Jefferson Street for the hoped-for victory party. The crowd that year was pretty rowdy even though we had lost. This year would be no exception. The police planned to do the same thing this year and we wanted to be at the heart of the celebration after we won the championship. My friends and I knew we had to be at Gatsby's no later that 6 P.M. for the 8 P.M. tip-off.

My friends came by my house around 5:30 that evening to pick me up. We got to Gatsby's around 6 o'clock and got a good table. There were six of us—me, my friend T. J. Johnson and his roommates Al Brown and John Long, and two guys I had met before, but didn't know well—Bob Myers and Butch Turner. Bob had gone to high school with T.J. Bob was in the Navy now and was stationed at Wayland, about 350 miles south of Nita City. Bob was on leave and had come with Butch, a friend in the Navy, to Nita City to visit T. J. As I said, I'd met these guys before but it was T. J. who knew them best. It didn't make a difference to me as we were all really excited about the game. We ordered some pizza and a couple of pitchers of beer right away before Gatsby's got busy. We finished the food and beer quickly and ordered two more pitchers before the game started. The

*The transcript of Lang's deposition was excerpted so that only his answers are reprinted here. Assume that this is a true and accurate rendering of those answers.

pitchers were advertised as being 48 oz. and that seemed about right. You would get about 6–8 glasses of beer out of each pitcher.

The first half was pretty close. We were up by a few points at halftime but our center was in foul trouble. Everyone was pulling for Nita U., except for Butch Turner. During halftime, we started talking about game strategies for the last half and complained about the TV commentators. We all thought Nita U. would win, though—that is, everyone but Butch. He was real outspoken about who he was for. When our team was down a couple of times during the first half, Butch would yell really loud. He got quite a few yells and dirty looks back. During halftime I noticed that he was acting really obnoxious. He was arguing about the game with the people at the table next to ours. Twice he shouted, "Go, Wildcats!" and then growled like a tiger. We told him to quiet down, but he ignored us. He had drunk more than his share of the four pitchers we'd ordered during dinner and the first half. I'd say that although he wasn't falling-down drunk, it was pretty obvious that Butch had been drinking. As I said, he was really being obnoxious about the game. He must have been a little drunk to pull so hard for State in a bar full of Nita U. supporters. I really felt sorry for our waitress because Butch had made a pass at her during the first half and was pestering her—wanting to go out with her after the game was over. He was also loudly predicting that Nita U. would lose. I suggested he put some money where his mouth was and we bet $25 on the game.

The second half started up and, as expected, the action was really good. We pulled ahead quickly and seemed to have a solid lead. Butch was quieter, but I noticed that he kept on drinking. We ordered two more pitchers as the second half began, just as the special price was about to go off. I had had about four glasses before that and was feeling pretty good, partly because of the beer, but mostly because we were playing so well. By the middle of the second half, Butch easily had drunk at least 1½–2 pitchers himself at the rate he had been going. His speech was getting slurred and he couldn't keep his hands off the waitress. It was with about four minutes left in the game that Butch ordered another two pitchers of beer. He paid for the beer himself but shared it with the table. But again, he was the primary consumer.

The game was really exciting during the last minute. Our center had sat out for at least five minutes when he got his fourth foul and the other team had pulled within two points. With ten seconds to go, we were down by one and our freshman guard was shooting a couple of free throws. He missed both and I knew the game was over. Butch went wild. He jumped on top of our table and began to chant "We're number one!" I tried to ignore Butch and just watched the screen. Several people shouted at him to shut up, and a waiter came over and told him to get off the table. Butch did, but almost slipped as he stepped onto the chair from the table.

By some miracle, we stole the ball, and a thirty-foot jumper won the game for us. Gatsby's literally rocked. Everyone was hugging each other and slapping each other on the back. People started dancing on the tables and throwing glasses on the floor. Butch had come down now, and I went over to him and made a crack that the game's not over until the last shot is in. I was just joking and didn't even mention the bet. But Butch took it all wrong and hit me in the stomach, and so I hit him back. Neither one of our punches had landed squarely and I wasn't interested in the fight—my team had just won—so I backed off and moved away from Butch. I then started to walk away, but he kept coming at me, and the last thing I remember was Butch's fist hitting my jaw before I fell to the floor.

When I came to, a policeman had come into Gatsby's. The owner was really upset. Several tables were broken, and glass was all over the floor. Our fight was the only fight in the place—most of the other students were celebrating the win and, by this time, were already on the street. The officer asked us how the fight started. I told him all I just told you, but Butch, of course, had his own version and said that I hit him first. That's just not true. The officer took our names and told us to go home. I guess he was more worried about controlling the crowd on Jefferson Street than handling small fights.

I tried to get up and join the celebration, but I was dizzy and couldn't stand without T. J.'s help. T. J. took me to the emergency room. I was hurt more than I thought I was. My stomach ached. I had a broken rib, some bruises, and a hairline fracture on the right side of my head. The doctors put me in the hospital to run some tests for a couple of days. I missed about a week and a half of classes and could not work at Simpson's for about two months—under doctor's orders.

My head hurt pretty bad for about two weeks after this. I would get a headache every day, usually in the afternoon. I also had trouble remembering things. The memory problems were real bad at first and after three weeks of trying to keep up with my classes, I had to withdraw for the spring YR-1 semester. At any rate, the headaches just got better over time, as did the memory problems. I wouldn't say the head and memory problems lasted more than two months.

It also took a couple of months to get over my broken rib. That was just real painful. I couldn't do anything without getting sharp pains in my rib cage. The doctor also kept me out of work for two months. When I work full time at Simpson's (which I do when I'm not in school), I make $160 in salary and another $250–$300 a week in tips. So I lost about $3,300–$3,700 at work. Also, people with my major are getting jobs in the $60,000 range, and I put that off for four months because I had to drop out for a summer while I got better physically. That cost me another $7,500 or so when you consider I could have been making compared to what I make at Simpson's.

On the way to the hospital, I did say to T. J. Johnson, "I guess I shouldn't have started the whole thing." But I didn't mean that I swung at Butch first. I only meant I probably should not have said anything about the game not being over until the last shot. Given all he had to drink and Butch's mood over his team losing, it was probably a stupid thing for me to have done.

I've been in some trouble in the past. My freshman year I was convicted of shoplifting. The store accused me of changing a price tag on a Polo dress shirt. The shirt cost $68.00, but the tag said $22.00. I didn't change the tag. Someone else must have done it or some clerk made a mistake tagging. I thought it was on sale. The detective claimed he saw me change tags, but that just wasn't true. The judge fined me $100 and put me on probation for one year. Two years ago I was also arrested for assault and battery. I got into a fight during a pick-up basketball game, but no one was hurt and the charges were dropped. Last year I was arrested for driving under the influence. I pleaded guilty and had to pay a fine and attend a safe driving course for two months. I haven't had any trouble since then until I was beaten up by Butch, and like I said, it wasn't my fault.

(This deposition was taken in the office of defendant's counsel on October 10, YR-1. After it was transcribed, it was signed by the deponent, Jeffrey Lang.)

JEFFREY LANG

Certified by:

ANNE DOLAN
Certified Shorthand Reporter (CSR)

DEPOSITION OF T. J. JOHNSON*

My name is T. J. Johnson. I was born May 20, YR-21, in Darrow City, Nita. I live at 37B University Apartments, Nita City, Nita. I am a senior at the University of Nita, majoring in Speech Communications.

I have known Jeff Lang for about four years now. I met him at a party my freshman year, and we've had some classes together since. I'd say we were pretty good friends. We have a lot in common. We both are avid basketball fans and usually go to the college games together. We had talked about going to New Orleans last March to see Nita U. play in the NCAA finals, but decided to stay in Nita for the parties after the game.

We decided to watch the game on the big screen TV at Gatsby's, a pizza parlor across from campus. I had a couple of friends come in unexpectedly for the game—Bob Meyers, a friend from high school who's now in the Navy, and Bob's friend, Butch Turner. I had kept in touch with Bob since graduation. He and Butch attended Nita Community College in Nita City for a couple of years before they decided to enlist. I saw a lot of Bob while he was at the Community College. I went to some of his parties and played on an intramural basketball team with him for two years. Butch was on the team also. I did not care much for Butch because he had a bad temper—he would yell at the referees over even minor calls. Though he was a good athlete, he was an aggressive player. Off the court, he was just as wild. He was a heavy drinker, and it was not unusual for him to pick fights with Nita U. students in local hangouts. Pretty much every time we'd go to a game, Butch would drink too much and start something. Evidently he hadn't changed since joining the service either. Bob told me that Butch had come close to being discharged for disciplinary problems.

It was about 6 P.M. when we all got to Mr. Gatsby's. I picked up Jeff at his parents' and we went right over. My roommates had gone to Gatsby's earlier to save us a table. We hadn't eaten yet, so we ordered some pizza and two or three pitchers of beer. Gatsby's had a special on beer, $2.00 for a 48 oz. pitcher. They were hoping, I guess, that a lot of students would come in to watch the game.

Everything was going pretty good until halftime. We probably had six pitchers between us by then, but I noticed that Butch seemed to be drinking twice as much as the rest of us. He wasn't falling down or anything, but he was real loud and real argumentative. He also was slurring his speech a little. He was flirting with the waitress and some girls at the next table. At one point he put his arm around the waitress and asked her to go out with him. She put him off nicely and went on to other tables. During halftime, Butch seemed to want to provoke a yelling match. He was saying that Nita U. was lucky that they were ahead, and the second half would be a different ballgame. He got into an argument about the game with a couple of guys at another table. I think it was sometime in there that Butch and Jeff argued about the game and I think they made a bet.

---

*The transcript of Johnson's deposition was excerpted so that only his answers are reprinted here. Assume that this is a true and accurate rendering of those answers.

We probably had four more pitchers of beer during the second half. Butch continued to pull against Nita U. and drank more than his share. But he also brought two pitchers for the table on his own, so no one was complaining. That purchase was sometime in the second half. At one point, when it looked like Nita State was going to win, Butch jumped on top of the table and shouted: "We're number one!" A waiter came over and told him to get off the table. Butch did, but almost slipped and fell.

Somehow we won on a last-second shot, and the place went crazy. People started screaming and jumping up and down. There was a lot of confusion—people were breaking glasses and turning tables over. Jeff went over to Butch and patted him on the back. I'm not exactly sure what Jeff said though, probably something about the game and their bet. But Butch hit Jeff in the stomach, and before I could stop them, they were rolling on the floor. The letters TJ show my position on exhibit E (see page 37) when the fight started. The letter F marks the spot where the fight was. Butch was facing and Jeff's back was to me when the fight started. Jeff got the worst of it before a policeman came to break up the fight. The officer was pretty decent about the whole thing—he didn't arrest anyone, just took down some names. The police knew there would be a lot of drinking downtown and were mainly trying to keep property damage down to a minimum. Jeff looked pretty bad, so I took him to the emergency room.

I'm pretty sure that Butch started the whole thing, but there were people jumping around and a lot of noise and confusion. On the trip to the hospital, Jeff did moan, "I guess I shouldn't have started the whole thing," but I don't think he meant he took a swing at Butch. Jeff's not that kind of guy. Anybody who knows Jeff would say the same thing. He's just not a violent guy.

Jeff was pretty messed up by this fight. For a couple months, he wasn't around at all. When I did see him I found out he had to drop out for the semester and couldn't even work at his job at Simpson's. Even though Jeff is a year older than me, he won't graduate until January of YR+1, six months after me.

(This deposition was taken in the office of defendant's counsel on October 12, YR-1. After it was transcribed, it was signed by the deponent, T. J. Johnson.)

T. J. Johnson

T.J. JOHNSON

Certified by:

Anne Dolan

ANNE DOLAN
Certified Shorthand Reporter (CSR)

DEPOSITION OF SUSAN CLARK*

My name is Susan Clark and I live at 314 Redwood Avenue, Nita City. I am twenty-five years old and have lived in Nita City all of my life. I am a waitress at Mr. Gatsby's, a restaurant on Jefferson Street in Nita City.

I had to work on the evening shift Monday, March 29, YR-1. That was the night of the NCAA basketball championship, with Nita U. vs. State. I came in early because we were expecting a full house. Gatsby's is primarily a college crowd restaurant. We had just gotten big screen TVs and had run a lot of ads hoping people would come in and watch the NCAA finals. We also had a special on beer to attract the students. We had a 48 oz. pitcher for $2.00 until 10:00 P.M.

We did have a policy that night of $5.00 per hour per table of four, for food and drink, but it wasn't really enforced. Everyone who came in and sat down ordered some pizza and beer and other things that night. The policy just let people know Gatsby's is a restaurant and not a lounge to sit and watch TV.

Things went pretty smoothly until the game started. People came early to get tables. By the time the game started, there were about 250–300 people in the place. There were six to eight people at most tables. I recognize the plaintiff from the picture you showed me. I know Jeffrey as someone who works at Simpson's restaurant. I've seen him at after-hours parties with people in my restaurant and by himself. I've never really talked to him, but I've seen him around. He seems like a nice enough guy. I waited on the plaintiff and his friends that night. They ordered a couple of large pizzas and a pitcher of beer when they first came in and later ordered a third pizza. I don't remember anything unusual about their behavior before the fight. Everyone in the place was in a good mood.

One of the guys at the plaintiff's table, the one who was in the fight with the plaintiff, was trying to flirt with me while I took their order. He might have put his arm around me or asked me out. I thought it was no big deal—you get used to customers having a little fun and trying to be cute after a while. I didn't serve them that much beer either, probably just a couple of rounds during the whole game. The guy who flirted with me did order a couple of pitchers at one time. I remember that because he gave me a big tip, which is unusual on an $8.00 bill—especially in a college town. He was not drunk when he placed his order, no slurred speech—nothing. Because of the crowd, it was cash only that night, and we weren't running tabs, so it's possible that another waitress or waiter served them or that they went up to the bar themselves, but I don't think they did. I would not have served them if they were drunk. We have a policy at work against serving customers who look like they've had too much to drink.

I was pretty busy during the evening because I waited on ten tables. I did see the fight though. I was standing in the doorway separating the back TV room from the side room when the fight started.

*The transcript of Clark's deposition was excerpted so that only her answers are reprinted here. Assume that this is a true and accurate rendering of those answers.

The students were really excited over the last-second shot which won the game. Everybody started cheering and shouting. A few guys got pretty rowdy—breaking glasses, throwing things on the floor, and knocking over tables and chairs.

In the midst of the excitement, the plaintiff went over to the guy who'd been flirting with me earlier, and it looked like the plaintiff said something to the guy. The plaintiff was facing me and the other guy's back was to me. I have marked the diagram, Exhibit E (see page 37) with the letters SC to show where I was when the fight started. The letter F shows where the fight was. The guy sure said something back, and then the plaintiff hit him in the chest. The guy then hit the plaintiff back. They swapped a couple of blows before I went back to the kitchen to call the police.

No, I did not see the guy who hit the plaintiff get on the table and cheer for State. I was pretty busy and missed that if it happened. It was real noisy, but I do remember hearing someone during the game shout, "Go, Wildcats," a few times. The other people didn't like that at all. I don't remember seeing anyone get on a table. We had a meeting that morning at which the boss told us to watch out for anyone who appeared intoxicated and report it to her. If I had seen anyone on the table, I would have told them to get off and maybe told the boss.

(This deposition was taken in the office of plaintiff's counsel on September 26, YR-1. After it was transcribed, it was signed by the deponent, Susan Clark.)

Susan Clark

SUSAN CLARK

Certified by:

Roger Powell

ROGER POWELL
Certified Shorthand Reporter (CSR)

DEPOSITION OF JENNIFER L. ANDERSON*

My name is Jennifer L. Anderson and I am thirty-five years old. I live at 4011 Westbrook Lane, Nita City. I have a degree in business administration from the University of Nita. Up until two years ago, I was an accountant with a local C.P.A. firm. I'd always wanted to own my own business and had an interest in developing closer contacts with the University community. I decided to open a restaurant three years ago, a pizza place called Mr. Gatsby's. I ran the restaurant on the side for about a year. I felt that it would be a more prosperous venture if I ran the place full time. There was a need for a good pizza parlor close to campus. Gatsby's today is probably one of the favorite college restaurants in Nita City. We have good, reasonably priced food and drink, three big screen televisions, and I just put in some video games last month.

I remember the evening of March 29, YR-1, well. The University of Nita basketball team had made it to the NCAA finals, and the whole town could talk of nothing else. The merchants on Jefferson Street were pretty excited, too. We all hoped to make some money on the crowds that would fill the college bars to watch the game, and a championship did wonders for T-shirt sales. I had stepped up my advertising in the campus paper, pushing our big-screen TVs and a special on beer—a 48 oz. pitcher for $2.00—hoping to have a packed house, too. We had a cover charge of sorts—a minimum of $5.00 per hour per table of four—for food or drink. The local merchants were also aware of the vandalism risks. Store windows had been covered and security was increased to try to keep the crowd contained.

As I expected, every seat was filled that night, and the bar area was packed. There were 300–350 people in the place. I had to keep a guy at the door all evening to turn people away once the game started. I usually run the cash register in the evenings, but that night I tried to mingle with the crowd to make sure everyone was served.

I don't remember anything unusual about the group of guys at the plaintiff's table that evening. A couple of them were actually pulling for the other team—which is why I recall seeing them before the fight at all. One guy was a little boisterous, but none appeared intoxicated. In fact, I had called an employees' meeting the day before to remind my crew of our policy of not serving anyone who looked intoxicated. Our policy is to fire any employee who serves an intoxicated person, but I really hadn't had a problem with this in the past. Sure, some of the students have gotten rowdy in the past, but this sort of thing is expected with a student hangout. I knew the crowd would be larger and noisier than any in the past and just wanted all my employees to be prepared. We were cited only once by the Nita Liquor Commission in January YR-1 for serving an intoxicated person, a student. I fired that waiter, and remembering that incident, I stressed the policy to the employees and told them to watch out for anyone who appeared to be getting intoxicated and to watch for anyone who appeared to have difficulty walking, talking, etc.

*The transcript of Anderson's deposition was excerpted so that only her answers are reprinted here. Assume that this is a true and accurate rendering of those answers.

I was about 15–20 feet away from the plaintiff's table when the fight started. One of my bus boys was having a hard time getting through the celebrating crowd to get to the kitchen, so I was trying to help him out. I have marked the letters JA on the diagram marked Exhibit E (see page 37) to mark where I was when the fight broke out. The letter F shows where the fight was. Everybody was jumping up and down, and things were starting to get out of hand. I glanced over my shoulder just in time to see the plaintiff hit a guy. I pushed my way over to try to break the guys up, but they both fell on the floor and kept on at it. A policeman and I finally calmed them down. By this time most of the students had gone outside, and I let the officer handle the fight while I looked around the place at the damage caused by the crowd. I was closed for two days to clean up and replace the broken tables and dishes.

I was once arrested for, and charged with, obtaining property by false pretenses. In April, YR-4, I sold a car to a guy after I had the odometer turned back from 65,000 miles to 40,000 miles. I told him that the car only had 40,000 miles on it. Somehow he found out about the change from the mechanic and went to the police. After I gave him his money back, he decided not to prosecute.

(This deposition was taken in the office of plaintiff's counsel on September 21, YR-1. After it was transcribed, it was signed by the deponent, Jennifer Anderson.)

JENNIFER ANDERSON

Certified by:

ROGER POWELL
Certified Shorthand Reporter (CSR)

TRANSCRIPT OF DEPOSITION OF PHILIP TURNER
EXAMINATION BY PLAINTIFF'S ATTORNEY
IN PRESENCE OF DEFENDANT'S ATTORNEY

Q: State your name and age.

A: My name is Philip D. Turner, but they call me Butch. I'm twenty-two years old.

Q: How tall are you?

A: 6'1"

Q: How much do you weigh?

A: 230 lbs.

Q: What is your occupation?

A: I'm enlisted in the Navy.

Q: Where are you stationed?

A: Wayland.

Q: How long have you been in the Navy?

A: I enlisted two years ago.

Q: What did you do before enlisting?

A: I attended Nita Community College in Nita City for about a year and a half.

Q: Do you ever return to Nita City?

A: Yes, I enjoy going back to visit when I can because I still have some friends there—people I knew while attending Nita Community College.

Q: Where were you on March 29 of last year?

A: Nita City.

Q: What brought you to Nita City?

A: My buddy, Bob Myers and I were really lucky and got passes for a few days, so we decided to go visit friends in Nita City. Bob had also attended Nita Community College and he thought it would be fun to be in Nita.

Q: Your main reason for going to Nita City was the basketball game, is that correct?

A: No, I wasn't much of a Nita U. fan, especially because of the way the University students looked down on those of us who went to the Community College. But I wanted to get away from the barracks and so I told Bob I'd go along with him.

Q: Where did you stay while in Nita City?

A: We stayed with a guy Bob knew from high school, T. J. Johnson, a senior at the University of Nita.

Q: Did you know T. J. Johnson?

A: Yes—Bob, T. J., and I had played on the same recreation league basketball team three years ago.

Q: Now, turning your attention to the events on March 29, YR-1, how did you spend the evening?

A: Well, about six of us went downtown to watch the NCAA finals.

Q: Who were the other five people?

A: T. J. Johnson, Bob Meyers, T. J.'s roommates—I'm not sure of their names—and a friend of T. J.'s, Jeff Lang.

Q: Had you previously known Jeff Lang?

A: No.

Q: Where did you go to watch the game?

A: We went to Mr. Gatsby's, a pizza and beer place across the street from the Nita U. campus.

Q: Why did you go there?

A: It was the perfect location for the street party that would follow the game. Also, the food was good, the beer was on special, and the place had three big screen TV's.

Q: When did you get to Gatsby's?

A: A little before 6 P.M.

Q: What did you do when you arrived?

A: We got a table and ordered dinner and some beer.

Q: That was about 6 o'clock, is that right?

A: Yes.

Q: What did you order for dinner?

A: We ordered two large pizzas with the works when we came in. Later, maybe around half time, we ordered a third pizza. Someone, I think, got some peanuts and chips at some time.

Q: Do you recall what time the game was over?

A: 10:30 P.M.

Q: How many pitchers of beer were ordered between 6 P.M. and 10:30 P.M.?

A: I believe we ordered three or four pitchers during the entire game.

Q: How much of the three pitchers ordered by the table did you personally consume?

A: I would estimate that I drank three to four glasses of beer.

Q: How many ounces was that?

A: The glasses were pretty small. I'd say it was 18 to 24 ounces all together.

Q: So you drank three or four glasses of beer, 24 to 32 ounces, between 6 P.M. and 10:30 P.M., is that correct?

A: Yes

Q: Was three or four glasses what you usually drink?

A: No, usually I would have more to drink, basically up to a six-pack or so, but I was really too interested in the game to do any serious drinking. I was also interested in our waitress.

Q: Can you be more specific?

A: I decided to be real nice, and she seemed to enjoy the attention I was giving her, you know, just kidding with her and tipping real good. I hoped to get a date with her after the game.

Q: You watched the game on Gatsby's wide screen TV, is that correct?

A: Yes.

Q: And did anything unusual happen at your table during the game?

A: No, everything went fine for the entire game. The game was really close, though—right down to the last second. I had made a bet with Jeff mainly to get him off my back.

Q: Jeff Lang is who you're referring to?

A: Yes.

Q: Can you explain why making a bet with Jeff Lang would get him "off your back"?

A: Well, I was pulling for the other team, and I didn't mind admitting it, but Jeff took it as a personal insult. He kept nagging me to make a bet because he thought Nita U. was so great.

Q: What happened after the game was over?

A: The minute it was over, Jeff Lang came over to me and immediately started bragging about winning and telling me to pay up. I started to reach in my back pocket for my wallet when Jeff pushed me. I was surprised, but before I could say anything, he hit me in the chest.

Q: Did you do anything in response?

A: I decided to give him a taste of his own medicine and hit him back. But he kept hitting back and jeering at me.

Q: How did the fight end?

A: The police came to break us up. I guess our fight got a bit rough. Anyway, the officer must have been used to college bar scenes, because he just took our names and told us to go home.

Q: Do you know what happened to Jeff Lang after the police broke up the fight?

A: I heard he had to be treated at the hospital that evening. I am sorry it happened, but I would not have hit him if he had not hit me first.

Q: What did you do after the fight?

A: I left the place and joined the crowd outside.

Q: Did you stand on the table that night?

A: Yes, I guess I did get a little carried away in the excitement of the game. But I got off when a waiter told me to.

Q: When was it that you stood on the table?

A: About midway through the second half.

Q: Did you order any beer after that time?

A: Yes. I ordered a pitcher for our table a little after that. I remember the waitress was grateful for the tip I gave her.

Q: Have you ever had trouble with the police before this incident?

A: Yes, three years ago, I was arrested for assault and battery at a Nita City bar. My attorney worked out a plea bargain arrangement so that I pled guilty and was convicted of drunk and disorderly conduct.

Q: Anything else?

A: Yes, two years ago, I pled guilty to shoplifting. A couple of friends and I took a case of beer from a store. When we were caught, we tried to claim we paid for it, but it didn't work. I was also arrested during a fight after a Nita U. football game that same year, but the charges were dropped.

Q: Have you had any disciplinary problems in the Navy?

A: I've been reprimanded for back talking my superior officer.

Q: Do you have any problems with other people in the Navy?

A: I've also had some problems getting along with individuals on my ship.

Q: Do you, or did you, drink alcohol on a regular basis?

A: Well, I guess I've had a drinking problem in the past.

Q: What kind of drinking problem?

A: When I drank, I would get a little belligerent and get into fights. Nothing serious, no weapons or anything—just fists.

Q: How regularly would this happen?

A: Every time I drank beer.

Q: How often was that?

A: Every free night I had, out drinking with friends.

Q: Was this behavior ongoing in May or June of YR-1?

A: Yes. I started getting some help through my commander at the base that fall. I attend meetings at the base and onboard when we are at sea.

(This deposition was taken in the office of plaintiff's counsel on September 26, YR-1. After it was transcribed, it was signed by the deponent, Philip D. Turner.)

Philip D. Turner

PHILIP D. TURNER

Certified by:

Roger Powell

ROGER POWELL
Certified Shorthand Reporter (CSR)

EXHIBIT A

University Hospital
Nita City, Nita

<u>Statement of Account</u>

Patient: Jeffrey B. Lang
141 Tarheel Drive
Nita City, Nita

Emergency Room (3/29/YR-1)	$750.00
Private Room Charge (3/29-4/1/YR-1)	3,600.00
Radiology Consultation	200.00
X-Rays	420.00
Laboratory	625.00
Pharmacy	285.00
Radiology (CAT Scan) (3/30/YR-1)	840.00
Attending Physicians	<u>925.00</u>
	$8,145.00

EXHIBIT B

Phillip Tromper, M.D., F.A.C.S.
131 Hancock Street
Nita City, Nita

To: Mr. Jeffrey B. Lang
141 Tarheel Drive
Nita City, Nita
4-28-YR-1

Statement for Professional Services

Treatment for rib fracture and head injuries

March 30–April 12, YR-1 $1,045.00

EXHIBIT D

UNIVERSITY HOSPITAL
Nita City, Nita

PATIENT:	Jeffrey B. Lang 141 Tarheel Drive Nita City, Nita	**D.O.B.** January 15, YR-22 **Employer:** Student-N.U. Simpson's Restaurant 12 Madison Lane Nita City, Nita	
N.O.K.:	Mrs. Rowan B. Lang 4809 Pine Street Nita City, Nita		
INS:	Nita State Student Plan	**ADMITTED:**	3/29/YR-1 11:32 p.m.

3/29/YR-1
11:32 p.m. ER Patient arrived via private car drive companion. Patient reports headache and dizziness after being knocked to floor in fist fight. Also reports being punched in abdomen and jaw. Bleeding from scalp. Tender in mid left abdomen and rib cage. Multiple bruises—abdomen, ribs, and face. B.P. 140/90. Resp. 20. Temp. 98.8. Pulse 80. Blood alcohol level .13%. Typed and cross matched. 3 sutures to scalp laceration. Full skull and abdomen series ordered stat.

A. Egan, M.D.

3/30/YR-1
1:45 a.m. Skull and abdominal series as per Egan order. Skull positive, hairline fracture right skull 6 cm. above ear socket, extending horizontally 3 mm. into right rear hemisphere. Abdominal positive, left eighth true rib. Clean fracture, 2 mm. left of intersection shaft and costal cartilage.

E. Shepherd, Technician

3/30/YR-1
2:15 a.m. Rib cage wrapped. Patient complains of pain in area of rib fracture and of headache. Aspirin-with-codeine tablets as needed for pain. No ambulation until further observation.

A. Egan, M.D.

3/30/YR-1 8:45 a.m.	Patient awakened from sound sleep. Unwrapped rib cage and examined for organ trauma. Examination negative. Re-wrapped rib cage using bi-fold tricolate tape. Patient complains of dizziness upon standing. B.P. 120/80. Resp. 20. Pulse 80. Temp. 98.5. CAT scan (brain) ordered stat. Continue aspirin-with-codeine as needed. Not to leave bed.

P. Tromper, M.D.

3/30/YR-1 1:00 p.m.	CAT scan as per Tromper order negative

T. Macon, Technician

3/30/YR-1 4:00 p.m.	Patient alert and resting comfortably. No dizziness. Pupils normal. Complains of slight headache. Continue medication and observation.

P. Tromper, M.D.

3/31/YR-1 9:01 a.m.	Patient awake. Vital signs normal. Complains of stiffness in left side and in jaw. Headache diminished. May leave bed within room. Medication as needed. Continue observation.

P. Tromper, M.D.

3/31/YR-1 4:45 p.m.	Progress good. Discontinue medication unless needed to aid in sleep.

P. Tromper, M.D.

4/1/YR-1 8:45 a.m.	Satisfactory progress. Discharge at 1:00 p.m. Complete home rest for one week. No physical labor for two months. Remove scalp sutures in 10 days. See patient as needed.

P. Tromper, M.D.

Certified as a true and correct copy of permanent records of University Hospital, Nita City, Nita.

[signature]

Allen Alden
Director, Medical Records
University Hospital

EXHIBIT D

SIMPSON'S RESTAURANT
12 Madison Land
Nita City, Nita

June 24, YR-1

To whom it may concern:

Jeffrey B. Lang was employed part-time by Simpson's Restaurant on March 29, YR-1. His job description was Food Server (waiter), and he was paid $4.00/hour plus tips.

Mr. Lang received no income from this restaurant during the two months leave of absence he took after being injured at Gatsby's Restaurant. As a part-time employee, he did not qualify for sick leave benefits, vacation pay, or our health care plan. He did not work full time for us during school breaks—working 5–8-hour shifts.

To determine Mr. Lang's estimated lost income from paychecks and tips during his two-month absence, we used our figures for tips declared by servers at the end of each shift from March 30, YR-1 to June 1, YR-1. During this period, the average amount of tips earned by a server was $40.00 on a weeknight and $70.00 on a weekend night. Mr. Lang worked two weeknight shifts and one weekend shift a week. Each shift is, on the average, seven hours long.

Mr. Lang would have earned an estimated $234.00 a week, including his income from paychecks and tips, had he been working for us in April and May, YR-1. Therefore, his estimated total gross pay for the eight weeks he was gone is $1,872.00. If Mr. Lang had worked full time during that same period, he would have worked two weekend and three weekday shifts and earned approximately $3,200. In addition, he would have earned benefits valued at 100% of his income.

Please do not hesitate to call me if you have any further questions.

Sincerely,

Pam J. Fields

Pam J. Fields
Assistant Manager

PJF/acn

EXHIBIT E

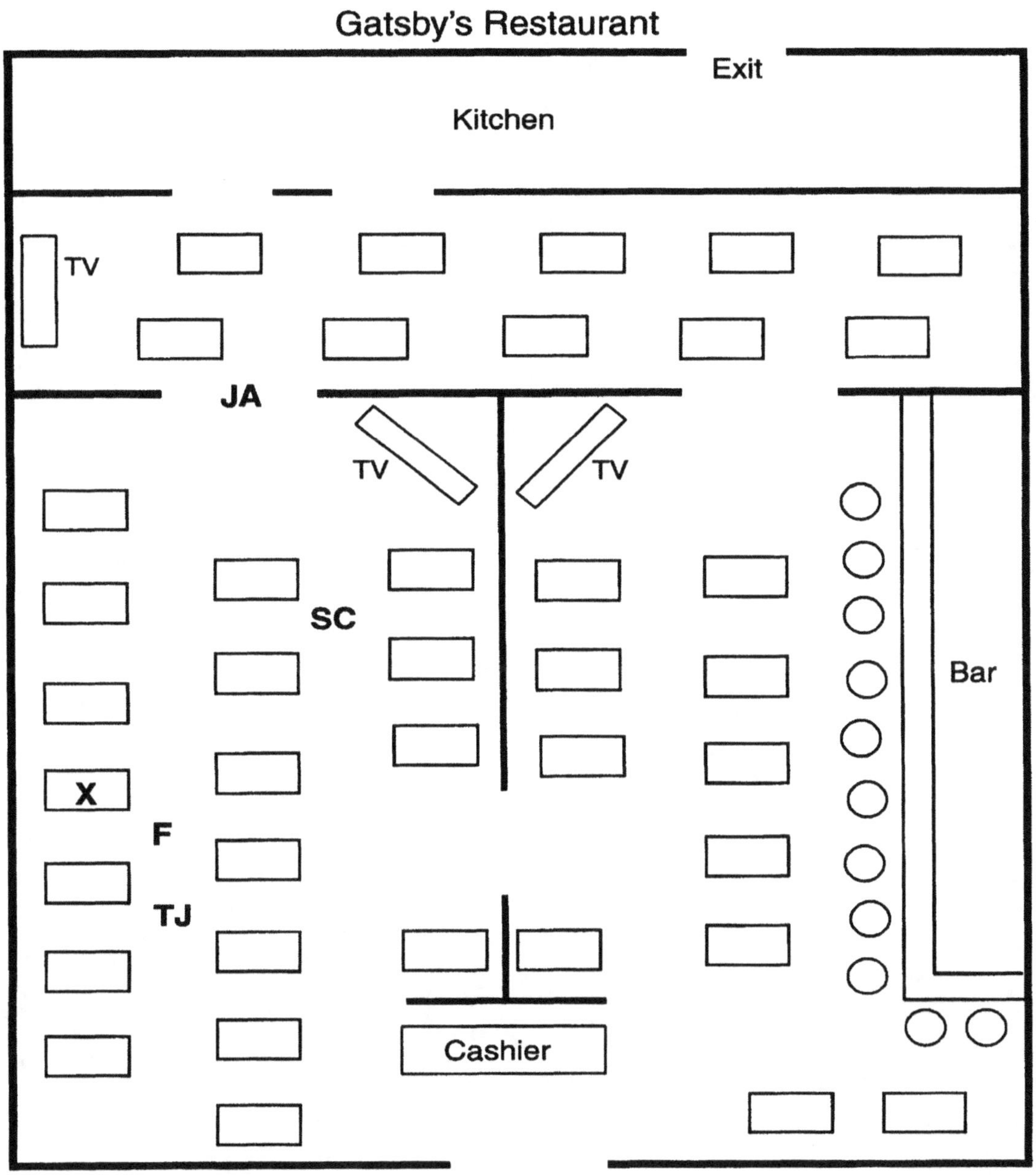

F Location of fight
X Plaintiff's table
JA Anderson's location when fight began
SC Clark's location when fight began
TJ Johnson's location when fight began

PUT ON THE RITZ
AT
MR. GATSBY'S
(A GREAT PLACE TO BE)

NCAA CHAMPIONSHIP SPECIAL
Monday Night 8 PM

UNIVERSITY OF NITA
VS.
NITA STATE

—See it on our Wide Screen TV!—

Pizza, Sandwiches, Good food
and
The Great Gatsby's Pitcher

(Championship Special's $2.00 per pitcher, Min. $5.00/hr. per table of four, 6–10 p.m.)

(This is a copy of a poster which appeared in the front window of Mr. Gatsby's. The poster was placed there on Sunday and it measured 2' x 4'.)

EXHIBIT F

...streak of under-par golf ...ld off a persistent Karrie ...a one-stroke victory in the ...n Open.

...pletes giant-killing

...co Clavet claimed one fi-...best.

...year-old Spaniard defeated ...hird-seeded Magnus Nor-... 6-2 Sunday to win the ... Templeton Classic, his ...court title in 13 years of ...nal tennis.

...is the happiest day in my ...," Clavet told the crowd af-... "I will keep these people ...ournament in my heart all

...g steady and waiting for ...nents to make mistakes, ...egan his week with an up-... 2 Andre Agassi, then beat ...g champion Lleyton He-... No. 4 seed on Saturday to ...to the finals.

... who has seven clay court titles. "To beat three players in the top 10 is like a dream to me."

Clavet is the 16th different winner — and the oldest — in 19 ATP tournaments this season. The $54,000 winner's purse was the second-biggest of Clavet's career.

Gambill wins Citrix

Jan-Michael Gambill had 11 aces and never lost his serve, beating Xavier Malisse 7-5, 6-4 to win the Citrix Tennis Championships on Sunday.

The fourth-seeded Gambill, off to the best start of his six-year career, takes home the $46,000 first prize. In six tournaments this year, he has reached three quarterfinals, a semifinal and becomes the 18th player in 19 tournaments to win a title this year.

With the victory, the 23-year-old American should crack the top 20 for the first time in his career. Gambill's only other title came in Scottsdale, Ariz., in 1999.

... cut down the nets.

In addition to their post-season success, this group also helped Penn complete an undefeated campaign at the Penn Palace this season and only one setback (Merrillville) at home during the past two years.

"The more times you win, the sweeter it gets because things only get harder and tougher after the first one," Foster said. "I am just so proud of this group because they are focused and are playing with such great discipline, composure, ..."

The Kingsmen continue their quest toward a state championship Wednesday night against Portage in the regional finals. Tip-off is set for 8 p.m. (South Bend time) at Portage High School.

Back on the war path

Winamac coach Brian Williams didn't mind seeing his squad get a little defensive this past weekend.

In winning their first sectional ti-...

... forgot," Mosson said. "They (Westview) are a much better team than their record (13-16) shows and our players showed a lot of mental toughness by being able to accomplish what we did in such a tough environment like Westview."

Glenn looks to make history Tuesday night at 7 p.m. when it hosts Central Noble for the regional championship.

A triple play

NorthWood accomplished quite a feat in winning its first Class 3-A sectional title since 1986 and second in the school's history.

In beating No. 10 Lakeland (63-56), Angola (70-59), and Northridge (64-54), the Panthers (18-5) avenged three of their five losses this season.

Despite playing all of the games on their home floor, the Panther Pit, NorthWood was the visiting team in each contest.

EXHIBIT G

Portions of the Interrogatories Answered by the Defendant

15. Please state the dollar amount of the gross sales of food and beverages by Mr. Gatsby's on the following Mondays for the second shift, 6:00 p.m. to 2:00 a.m.:

February 22, YR-1	$843.85
March 1, YR-1	$798.54
March 8, YR-1	$851.24
March 15, YR-1	$810.19
March 22, YR-1	$901.87
March 29, YR-1	$2,945.92
April 5, YR-1	$788.88
April 12, YR-1	$856.93
April 19, YR-1	$801.01
April 26, YR-1	$814.19

* * * *

25. Please state whether Mr. Gatsby's has insurance covering any liability that might arise under the Nita Dramshop Act? Yes

26. If the answer to interrogatory 25 is yes, please state the name and address of the insurer and the liability limits of the policy.

Temperance Insurance Company
404 Basil Road
Nita City, Nita 00001

The policy limits are: $1,000,000 per incident
$500,000 per person

EXHIBIT H

UNIFORM ARREST AND DISPOSITION RECORD

NAME: Jeffrey B. Lang		**DOB:** 1/15/YR-22	
S.S. NO. 456-88-5994		**POB:** Nita City, Nita	
DATE	**ADDRESS**	**OFFENSE**	**DISPOSITION**
10/5/YR-4	214 Branch Hall Univ. of Nita Nita City, Nita	Petit Larceny 10 Nita GS Sec. 23(a)(4)-Changing Price Tags	Guilty Fine $100 Probation 1 yr.
3/18/YR-3	68 Tarheel Dr. Apt. D Nita City, Nita 9(c)	Assault & Batt. 10 Nita GS Sec.	Dismissed with leave
1/1/YR-2	68 Tarheel Dr. Apt. D Nita City, Nita	DUI (.19) 10 Nita GS Sec. 54(b) Costs	Plea of Guilty, Fine $300 Probation 1 yr. Safe Dr. C., 3 mon. suspen. lic.

Certified as of the 24th day of October YR-1

John Schnek
Superintendent of Documents

Notary Public

EXHIBIT I

UNIFORM ARREST AND DISPOSITION RECORD

NAME: Philip D. Turner a.k.a. Butch Turner — **DOB:** 4/5/YR-22

S.S. NO. 600-44-3333 — **POB:** Flint, Nita

DATE	ADDRESS	OFFENSE	DISPOSITION
2/15/YR-4	400 S. Ram Ave. Nita City, Nita	Assault & Batt. 10 Nita GS Sec. 12(a)	Dismissed w/o leave
		Drunk & Dis. 10 Nita GS Sec. 9(c)	Plea Guilty Fine $100 Attended AA class
10/8/YR-4	400 S. Ram Ave. Nita City, Nita	Assault & Batt. 10 Nita GS Sec. 9(c)	Dismissed w/leave
11/5/YR-2	400 S. Ram Ave. Nita City, Nita	Petit Larceny 10 Nita GS Sec 23(a)(2)	Plea Guilty Fine $50 1 yr. probation

Certified as of the 24th day of October YR-1

John Schnek
Superintendent of Documents

Notary Public

EXHIBIT J

UNIFORM ARREST AND DISPOSITION RECORD

NAME: Jennifer L. Anderson		**DOB:** 1/2/YR-35	
S.S. NO. 146-88-9110		**POB:** Nita City, Nita	
DATE	**ADDRESS**	**OFFENSE**	**DISPOSITION**
4/18/YR-4	4011 Westbrook Ln. Nita City, Nita	Obtaining property by false pretense 10 Nita GS Sec. 344(b)(3)	Dismissed w/leave

Certified as of the 24th day of October YR-1

John Schnek
Superintendent of Documents

Notary Public

EXHIBIT K

MEMORANDUM

To: Senior Partner

From: Clerk

Re: Lang v. Anderson; Liability under the Nita Dramshop Act

Facts: Jeffrey B. Lang, Plaintiff, has retained our services to bring a lawsuit against Jennifer L. Anderson, owner of Gatsby's Restaurant of Nita City, Defendant. Lang was injured by Butch Turner, an intoxicated customer of Anderson's, in a fight following the YR-1 NCAA championship game. This memorandum reviews the possible liability of Anderson under the Nita Dramshop Act.

Discussion: The Nita Dramshop Act imposes liability without fault upon one who, by selling or providing alcohol, causes a person to become intoxicated, and the intoxicated person injures another's person, property, or mental state. In a recent decision, Beale v. Jones, 431 Nita 315 (2000), the Nita Supreme Court set forth the elements of a prima facie case for a dramshop action. First, the plaintiff must show that intoxicating liquor was served by the defendant to the person accused of injuring the plaintiff. The plaintiff must next show that the liquor served by the defendant caused the person to be intoxicated. Third, the Plaintiff must show that the person served alcohol must have been visibly intoxicated at the time he or she was served alcohol. Finally, the plaintiff must prove that a direct, affirmative, tortious act by the intoxicated person had a causal connection with the injuries sustained by the plaintiff.

In establishing the case, there are several issues which require particular attention. First, Plaintiff must show that Butch Turner was intoxicated. The Nita State courts have generally defined intoxication as the consumption of alcohol, resulting in the impairment of the consumer's mental and physical faculties and diminution in his ability to think and act with ordinary care. Because of the wide variances in individual tolerances for alcohol, in dramshop cases the Nita courts require the plaintiff not only to show that the allegedly intoxicated person consumed alcohol, but also to show independent evidence that the person was in fact intoxicated. Such independent proof would include evidence of unusual or erratic behavior. See Brown v. Blake, 394 Nita 111 (1998).

In addition to showing that Turner was intoxicated, Plaintiff must also prove that the beer consumed at Gatsby's was not merely a "negligible amount," but that the beer was a material and substantial factor in producing or contributing to produce intoxication and the resultant injury to the plaintiff." Neese v. Sloop, 392 Nita 446, 449 (1998). In Neese, the Nita Supreme Court stated that the factors to be considered in determining whether the alcohol served at an establishment was a material and substantial element causing the plaintiff's injury include not only the amount of alcohol consumed at the establishment, but also:

1. lapse of time;

2. the number of other factors which contributed to producing the harm and the extent of their contribution; and

3. whether the defendant's conduct created a force or series of forces which were in continuous and active operation up to the time of the harm.

Neese, 392 Nita at 450.

While the facts of the case should establish the elements of a dramshop action, the facts also raise the defense Provocation. The Dramshop Act itself sets forth the defense of Provocation to an action under the statute. In addition, the Nita courts have long held that one who is not an "innocent suitor" would be barred from recovery. Aiker v. King, 123 Nita 231 (1960).

Jones v. Post, 249 Nita (1985).

In Wilson v. Stark, 291 Nita 510 (1990), the Nita Supreme Court discussed the affirmative defense of Provocation in a dramshop case. The court stated that the defense has the burden of proving that the plaintiff provoked the tortious act which injured the plaintiff.

PROPOSED JURY INSTRUCTIONS

1. The Court will now instruct you on the law governing this case. You must arrive at your verdict by unanimous vote, applying the law as you are now instructed to the facts as you find them to be.

2. As you know, the plaintiff, Jeffrey B. Lang, seeks to recover damages based upon a claim that the defendant, Jennifer L. Anderson, owner of Mr. Gatsby's Restaurant, by serving and selling alcoholic beverages to Butch Turner, caused the intoxication of Butch Turner, and that Butch Turner injured the plaintiff while in this intoxicated condition.

   The defendant denies that, as a result of the beer consumed at Mr. Gatsby's Restaurant, Butch Turner became intoxicated. The defendant claims that the plaintiff provoked the fight with Turner. The defendant asserts that she, therefore, is not liable for the plaintiff's injuries.

3. The Nita Dramshop Act provides that anyone who is injured in person, property, or otherwise, by an intoxicated person, has a right of action against any person, who by selling or giving away alcoholic beverages, causes the intoxication of the one who commits the injury.

4. In order to recover on this dramshop action, the plaintiff has the burden of proving the following propositions:

   (a) That the person who injured the plaintiff was intoxicated;

   (b) That a direct, affirmative, wrongful act by the intoxicated person caused the plaintiff to be injured;

   (c) That an intoxicating liquor was served by the defendant, through her employees, to the person accused of injuring the plaintiff;

   (d) That at the time of service of intoxicating beverages, the person was visibly intoxicated;

   (e) That the intoxicating beverage served by the defendant was a material and substantial factor in producing or contributing to the person's intoxication, and the resultant injury to the plaintiff.

   If the above propositions are proven, the defendant is liable to the plaintiff even though she exercised all possible care in the serving and sale of alcoholic beverages to the patrons of her restaurant.

5. Service of Intoxicating Beverages. The defendant has admitted that she, through her employees, served Butch Turner intoxicating beverages. Therefore, you must take this fact as proven since it is not an issue in the case.

6. Factual Issues for the Jury. The factual issues you are to determine are as follows:

(a) Whether Butch Turner was in fact intoxicated;

(b) Whether a direct, affirmative, and wrongful act by Butch Turner caused the plaintiff's injuries;

(c) Whether the intoxicating beverages served by the defendant, through her employees, was a material and substantial factor in producing:

(1) Butch Turner's intoxication, and

(2) The resultant injuries to the plaintiff Jeffrey Lang;

(d) Whether Turner was visibly intoxicated when he was served intoxicating beverages by the Defendant;

(e) Whether the plaintiff provoked the fight with Butch Turner; and

(f) What, if any, damages the plaintiff sustained as a result of the injuries.

7. Intoxication. A person is intoxicated when he has consumed a quantity of alcohol sufficient to cause loss of normal control of either bodily or mental faculties, or both, to such an extent that there is a diminished capacity to think and act with ordinary care. The plaintiff must prove independent evidence that Turner was in fact intoxicated. Independent evidence would include evidence of amount of alcohol consumed, erratic or unusual behavior, and any other relevant factors.

8. Material and Substantial Factor. If you find that Butch Turner was visibly intoxicated and that a direct, affirmative, and wrongful act by Butch Turner caused the plaintiff's injury, then you must next determine whether the alcohol consumed by Butch Turner at Mr. Gatsby's was a substantial and material factor in producing or contributing to Butch Turner's intoxication and the injuries sustained by the plaintiff, Jeffrey Lang. A "material and substantial factor" is one that has some bearing on the outcome of an event. In determining this issue you may consider:

(a) the amount of alcohol consumed by Butch Turner at Mr. Gatsby's;

(b) the amount of time that elapsed between the consumption of the alcohol and the act which injured the plaintiff;

(c) other factors which contributed to producing the harm and the extent of their contribution; and

(d) whether the service of intoxicating beverages to Butch Turner created a force or series of forces which were in continuous and active operation up to the time of the harm to the plaintiff.

9. Direct, Affirmative, and Wrongful Act. If Butch Turner struck the plaintiff without legal justification, you are to find that the act was a direct, affirmative, and wrongful one.

10. Defendant's Affirmative Defense. The defense of Provocation of the wrongful act which injured the plaintiff is available to the defendant, Jennifer Anderson, on the plaintiff's claim of dramshop liability. The defendant has the burden of proof on each of the defenses.

11. Provocation. The defendant contends that the plaintiff provoked the wrongful act which resulted in his injury. In order for you to find Provocation, the defendant must show that the plaintiff, by conduct or actions, willingly incited or enraged Butch Turner and thereby caused the latter to injure the plaintiff.

12. If you find from all the evidence that the plaintiff has proven each of the elements necessary to establish a dramshop action and that the defendant has failed to prove either Complicity or Provocation, then your verdict shall be for the plaintiff. If, on the other hand, you find that any element of the plaintiff's claim has not been established or that the defendant has proven Complicity or Provocation, then your verdict shall be for the defendant.

13. If you find in favor of the plaintiff, Jeffrey Lang, then you must assess his damages and determine the amount of money that will fairly and adequately compensate him for his injures. The plaintiff has the burden of proof on damages. The plaintiff may recover for all damages that were proximately caused by the attack of Butch Turner resulting from Turner's intoxication. Proximate cause means a cause that, in a natural and continuous sequence, produces the injury. It is the cause without which the injury would not have occurred.

14. In determining the amount of damages sustained by the plaintiff, you should consider the following:

(a) The reasonable expense of necessary medical care;

(b) The value of any lost earnings;

(c) The physical pain, suffering, or discomfort experienced; and

(d) The emotional distress, humiliation, or lost reputation experienced.

In the Circuit Court
Darrow County, Nita
Civil Division

Jeffrey B. Lang, Plaintiff, vs. Jennifer L. Anderson doing business as Mr. Gatsby's Defendant.	))))))))	JURY VERDICT FORM # 1

We, the jury, return the following verdict and each of us concurs in this verdict:

(Choose the appropriate verdict)

I. We, the jury find for the plaintiff in the sum of $_____.

____
Foreperson

II. We, the jury, find for the defendant.

____
Foreperson

In the Circuit Court
Darrow County, Nita
Civil Division

Jeffrey B. Lang,	)	
Plaintiff,	)	
vs.	)	JURY VERDICT FORM # 2
	)	
Jennifer L. Anderson	)	
doing business	)	
as Mr. Gatsby's	)	
Defendant.	)	

We, the jury, return the following verdict and each of us concurs in this verdict:

(Choose the appropriate verdict)

I. We, the jury find for the plaintiff.

____
Foreperson

II. We, the jury, find for the defendant.

____
Foreperson

In the Circuit Court
Darrow County, Nita
Civil Division

Jeffrey B. Lang,	)	
Plaintiff,	)	
vs.	)	JURY VERDICT FORM # 3
	)	
Jennifer L. Anderson	)	
doing business	)	SPECIAL VERDICT
as Mr. Gatsby's	)	
Defendant.	)	

We, the jury, find and answer the questions below as follows:

1. Was Butch Turner intoxicated? _______

2. Did a direct, affirmative act of Butch Turner cause plaintiff's injuries? _______

3. Was the beer served by defendant Jennifer L. Anderson's employees to Butch Turner a material and substantial factor in producing Butch Turner's intoxication?

   ____

4. Was the beer served by defendant Jennifer L. Anderson's employees to Butch Turner a material and substantial factor in producing the injuries sustained by plaintiff Jeffrey B. Lang? _______

5. Did plaintiff Jeffrey B. Lang, by his conduct or action, willingly incite or enrage Butch Turner, thereby provoking Butch Turner to strike and injure him? _______

6. Did plaintiff Jeffrey B. Lang incur any damages as a result of Butch Turner striking him? _______

7. If plaintiff Jeffrey B. Lang did incur any such damages, the amount of the damages was:
   $_______

____
Foreperson

www.ingramcontent.com/pod-product-compliance
Lightning Source LLC
LaVergne TN
LVHW082359200926
848481LV00012B/3624